Foreword

I am delighted to have been asked to write the foreword to this book. It gives me the chance to acknowledge this innovative series of books created with, and for young carers by Sefton Carers Centre.

Although I consider myself lucky to have been highly successful in business, I have never forgotten my roots. Growing up I went to nine different schools and lived in nine different houses, many of which were in what today would be called disadvantaged areas of Liverpool. That upbringing certainly helped both shape me as a person and prepare me for my business life to come.

Having supported many charities on a personal level throughout my Redrow career, in 2001 I started the Foundation because I wanted to give back to society. I wanted to make a difference to the lives of people in the areas I was born and raised.

Most of all I want to help people coping with disability and disadvantage by supporting local charities that are doing practical things to help people; charities which have a real impact at the grass roots of society. Sefton Carers Centre is one such charity; the Foundation is pleased to be supporting the Young Carers Service.

Carers of all ages face many issues and challenges throughout their own lives and that of the person they care for. Young carers rarely see themselves as carers and don't often recognise the importance of their own lives and happiness. These books will enable young carers to identify with the central character, their day to day reality and the impact support can bring, whilst offering uplifting stories that are an inspiration to all.

The books are a fictional interpretation of the young carers stories, showing the super-human effort some young carers go through each day and also the difference the support, care and comradeship offered to young carers by the young carers project, professionals, schools, friends and family can make.

I hope that young carers will enjoy these books, seeing themselves in the central role and how with support they can continue caring with the confidence they are not alone.

Steve Morgan CBE
Founder and Chairman, Steve Morgan Foundation

WITH A CARE IN THE WORLD

anya

A Young Carer's story of caring for someone with Dementia

By Charles Lea
Illustrated by Andrew Mulvenna

A Note from Sefton Carers

Anya is a fictional young carer, but her story has been based on the real-life experiences of young carers who live in Sefton. Over Autumn 2019 author Charles Lea met with a number of these amazing young people and listened to what they had to say about their lives. From these accounts he wrote this story and three other stories about young carers who look after members of their family.

A Carer is anyone who helps look after someone in their family who is ill or has a disability. Sefton Carers Centre is a local charity who will listen and provide support to any carer who is over the age of 5.

There are many children out there, not only in Sefton, but throughout the United Kingdom and the world who care for their families and do not know of the support which Sefton Carers Centre, and other organisations, can give to them.

We hope all four of these stories show you just how young carers can be helped, as they, themselves, help others.

The other stories in the "With A Care in the World" collection are:

Evie — A young carer's story of caring for someone with Autism

Grace — A young carer's story of caring for someone with Mental Health Problems.

Rishi — A young carer's story of caring for someone with Cancer.

If you, a family member or friend, need help and support as a young carer you can contact Sefton Young Carers Team on 0151 288 6060 or e-mail help@carers.sefton.gov.uk. Information about Sefton Young Carers Service can also be found on website www.sefton-carers.org.uk.

carerstrust
Sefton
Carers Centre
action · help · advice

"With A Care in the World. Anya, a young carer's story of caring for someone with Dementia" first published 2020 by Sefton Carers Centre, 27 to 37 South Road, Waterloo, L22 5PE. Sefton Carers Centre is a registered charity in England and Wales, No: 1050808. Registered as a company limited by guarantee in England No: 3124430.

The right of Charles Lea to be identified as the author of this work has been asserted by him.

The right of Andrew Mulvenna to be identified as the illustrator of this work has been asserted by him.

ISBN Number 9781916340626

Copyright © 2020 Charles Lea

Illustrations Copyright © 2020 Andrew Mulvenna

Cover Design and Layout by Suzanne Green and Rob Russell

All rights reserved. This book is sold subject to the condition that it shall not, by way of trade or otherwise, be lent, hired out or otherwise circulated in any form of binding or cover other than that in which it is published. No part of this publication may be produced, stored in a retrieval system, or transmitted in any form or by any means (electronic, mechanical, photocopying, recording or otherwise) without the prior written permission of Sefton Carers Centre.

This is a work of fiction. Names, characters, incidents and dialogues are products of the author's imagination or are used fictitiously. Any resemblance to actual people, living or dead, events or otherwise is entirely coincidental.

Anya's Story

Some of my earliest memories of my life are with Mum, Dad and my Nanna on Southport Pier and the promenade. At the end of the pier you can see everything, from the beach and the sea right below your feet to miles all around.

Every time we go there now, I sense all those past times we have been. In fact, all I need is a sunny day and my imagination can take me there with all the smells of the sand and sea and candy floss and chips. I wish I was there now.

I absolutely adore my Nanna. She has the lovcliest smile and she is the best thing in the world since sliced bread which is what she used to give me when I was younger when she used to look after me. Sliced bread with butter. Proper bread too. I could have eaten the whole loaf.

Imagine my surprise and delight when I was told that she was going to come and live with us. I was so overjoyed. Our family, all living together under one roof.

That's four of us: Mum, Dad, Nanna and me. My name is Anya and I am 9 years old, almost 10.

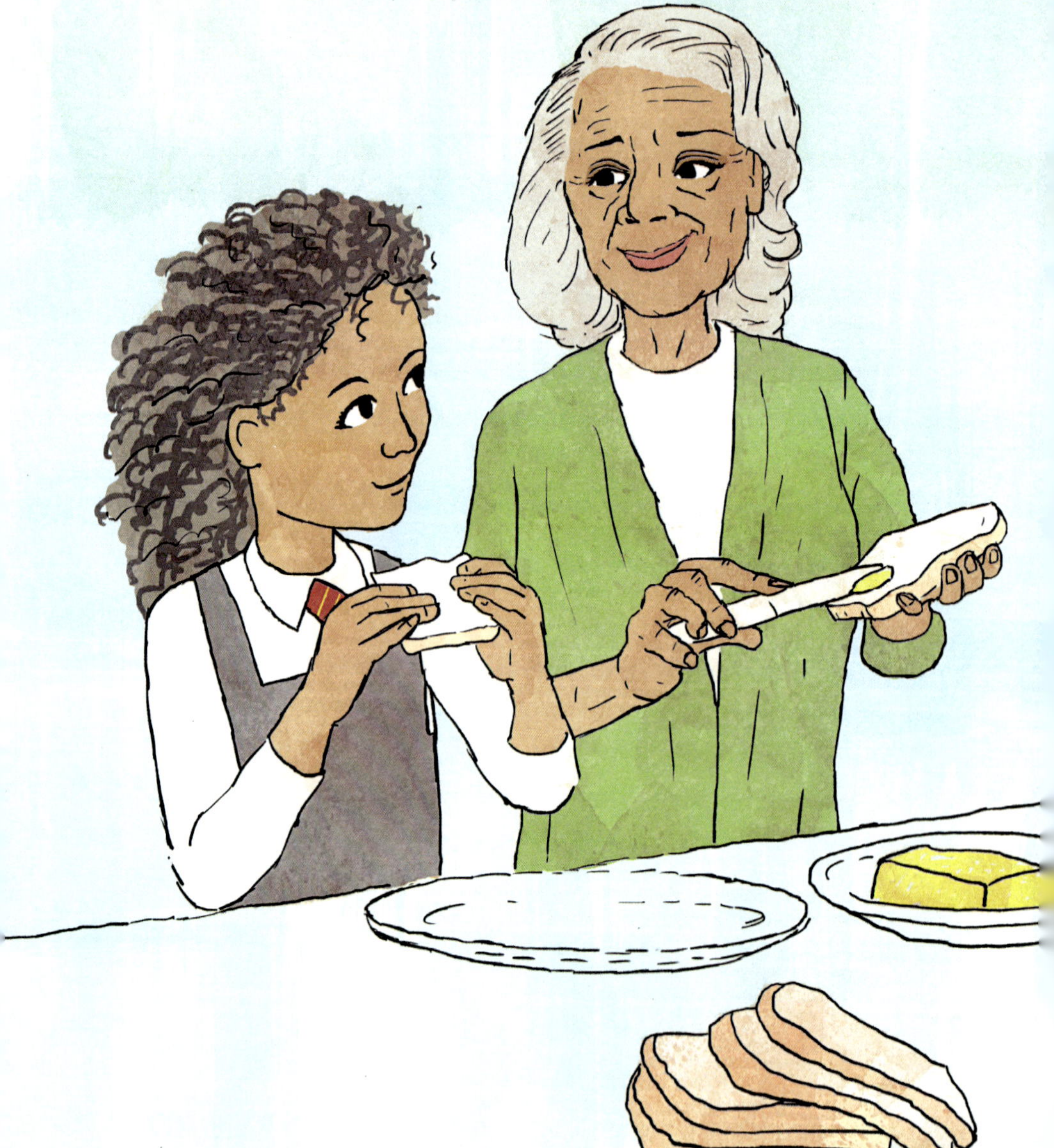

I used to love coming home from school and there would be Nanna, sitting in her armchair watching Countdown and then all the other quizzes on the telly. We would always have a cup of tea together, some bread and butter and, if we were lucky, some cake as well. Nanna had it all ready for when I got back home.

And then, at the weekend, whether it was sunny, rainy, windy or just plain cold, Dad would drive us all to Southport and we would have a few hours doing not very much but I loved it.

When it was sunny, and the tide was in I would have a paddle and make a sandcastle and Nanna would watch and say that I was her beautiful mermaid and she would ask, "Mermaid, what wish will you give me?"

And I would reply, "all the love in the world," and I would wiggle around as if I had a tail rather than legs.

"Thank you my dear," she would say and then she would cross my palm with gold, or rather a pound coin. I was rich! Sometimes, she would find a mermaid's purse on the beach and tell me to put the pound into the purse.

Later we would take the tram on the pier and go and have a cup of tea in the café, right at the end of it. Nanna would tell me all about the history of the pier and that she had played on it when she had been my age.

"Its one of the longest piers in the country," she would say, "and is the oldest one made of iron." She was so proud of the pier. Nanna would then go on about Southport back in her day and sing one of the old songs. "This was where your Grandad and I would do our courting," she would continue, "you call it dating now. He would be all dressed up in his finest clothes and he would walk me up and down the promenade and make me feel like I was the Queen."

And I would sit there and imagine Nanna and Grandad when they were young.

I also imagined that Nanna would be remembering all those good times too.

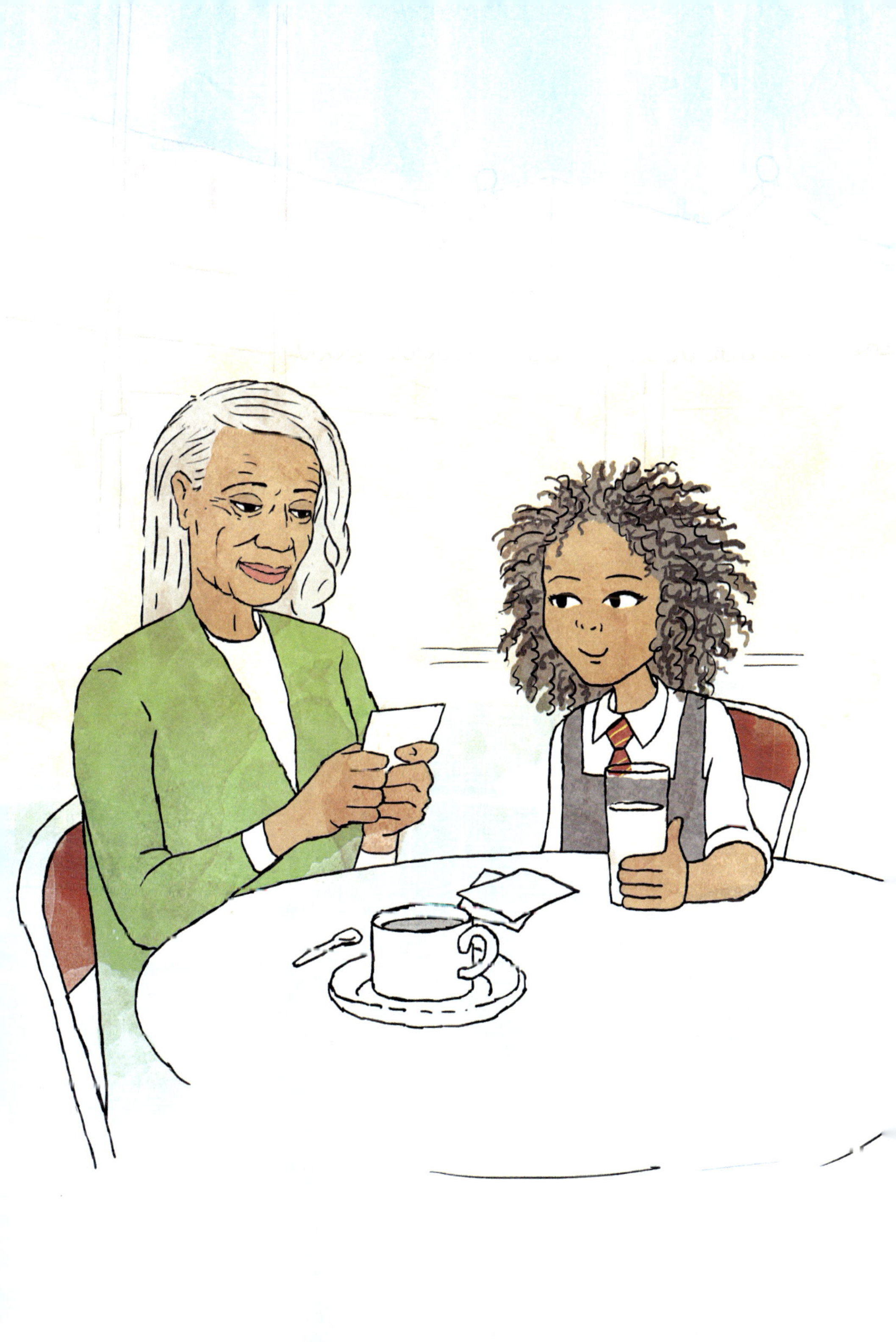

About a year ago, I noticed a bit of a difference with Nanna. It didn't feel like anything really, until Mum had a little chat to me.

I would get home from school and, of course, I would be starving and looking forward to bread and butter, but there wouldn't be any.

"Is there no bread and butter today Nanna?" I would ask.

And she would sit there thinking and then remember.

"Ooh, I quite forgot," she said, "let me sort it out now."

At about the same time, when I used to paddle on Southport beach, I would go up to her and say, "look Nanna, I am your mermaid, what wish do you want to me give you?" and I would wiggle around again.

But Nanna would just look at me, just like one of my teachers when I was being silly at school, as if to say, "what are you doing Anya?"

So, I would find her a mermaids purse and repeat, "I am your mermaid, what wish do you want me to give you?"

And, a few seconds later, she would remember and say, "all the love in the world," and she would smile at me.

I wasn't after the pound coin by the way, I just wanted to see her lovely smile.

That night, when Mum got home, I told her what had happened with Nanna.

Mum said that although I was a bit too young to understand, I had a right to know what was happening to Nanna. She told me Nanna had something called dementia and it meant that her memory was failing and that she was finding it difficult to do a lot of the everyday things that she used to do so well.

Mum told me that this was the reason Nanna had moved in with us, so we could help her. Mum did not want Nanna to be alone in her own home. It was also the reason we went out to Southport every weekend.

I told Mum that I would do all that I could to help my Nanna.

Within a few weeks Mum's work had said she could work less hours so she could spend more time with Nanna. It also meant that she could pick me up from school rather than my friend's mum drop me off.

Now that Mum was home more I thought everything would be fine. Nanna would not have to do as much and so there would not be any trouble.

I was wrong. Nanna's dementia got worse.

She had long stopped cutting bread for me or anyone else, but Nanna did not like having everything done for her and sometimes there would be a row between her and Mum. Nanna

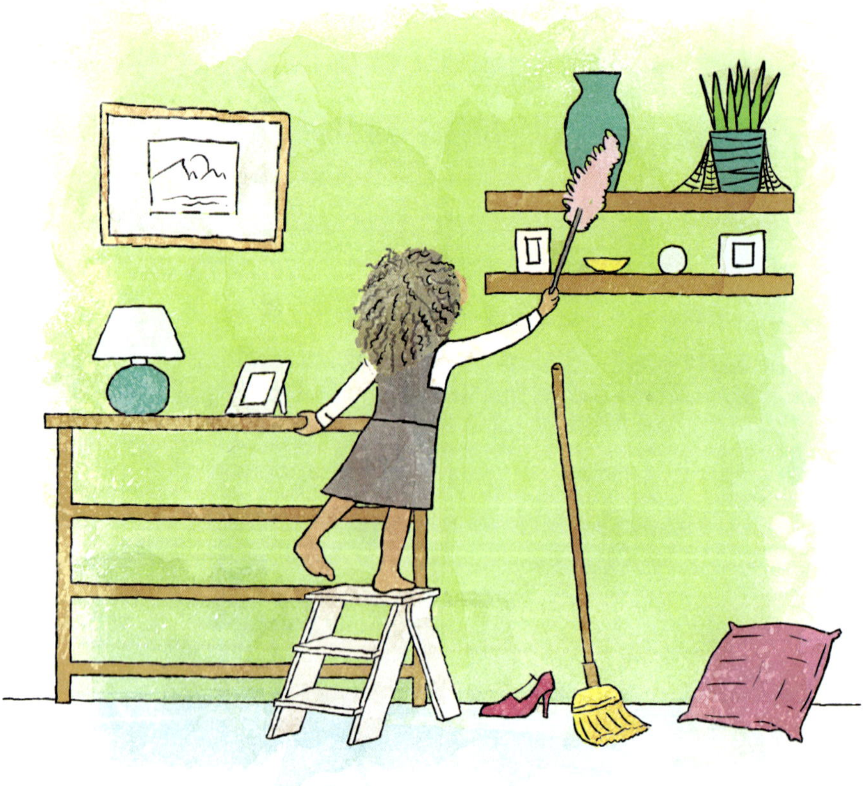

wanted to do things, like help clean and dust the house, wash the clothes or make the tea at night.

Mum told her that she didn't need to do those sorts of things anymore as she could do them. Mum was worried that Nanna could have an accident if she tried to do things around the house.

But I noticed that Mum was becoming ever more tired and that the cleaning and tidying weren't getting done all the time. I worried that Nanna might try and do them and that is when I had a brain wave. I could do them!

I started making sure my room was all clean but soon I started cleaning and dusting all over the house, even in the bathroom. But I had to do it, my bit, otherwise Nanna would try, and I didn't want her hurting herself.

It still wasn't the end of it.

At night-time I would often awake to hear things clatter around the house. At first I thought it was a burglar and was frightened but then I heard it was Nanna, downstairs and she seemed to be having a right good shout at something.

I remember, the first time it happened, I ran down to see what was happening and thank God I did.

Nanna was in the kitchen and she had boiled the kettle ready to make a hot water bottle. But her hands were shaking, and I knew she would spill the red-hot water onto her hands.

I ran towards her to stop her lifting the kettle and must have frightened the life out of her. She went mad at me and yelled all sorts of things and I got upset.

Thankfully, her shouting woke Mum and Dad who raced downstairs and sorted everything out.

From then on, me, Mum and Dad kept our bedroom doors open to help us listen if Nanna had gone downstairs. I tried to stay awake all night so I could hear her.

What with the trying to keep awake at night and helping Mum do lots of tidying, I felt shattered in the morning.

I did not really want to go to school as I was so tired. By the time it got to the afternoon lessons, after lunch, I was often falling asleep.

It became a bit of a joke in class, but it was no joke to my teacher.

I was getting into trouble.

At the weekend or on school holidays it has become difficult to do some of the things I want to do. Mum isn't earning as much as she used to so we have less money to spend on nice things and we also must take Nanna with us wherever we go too, she simply cannot be left on her own in the house.

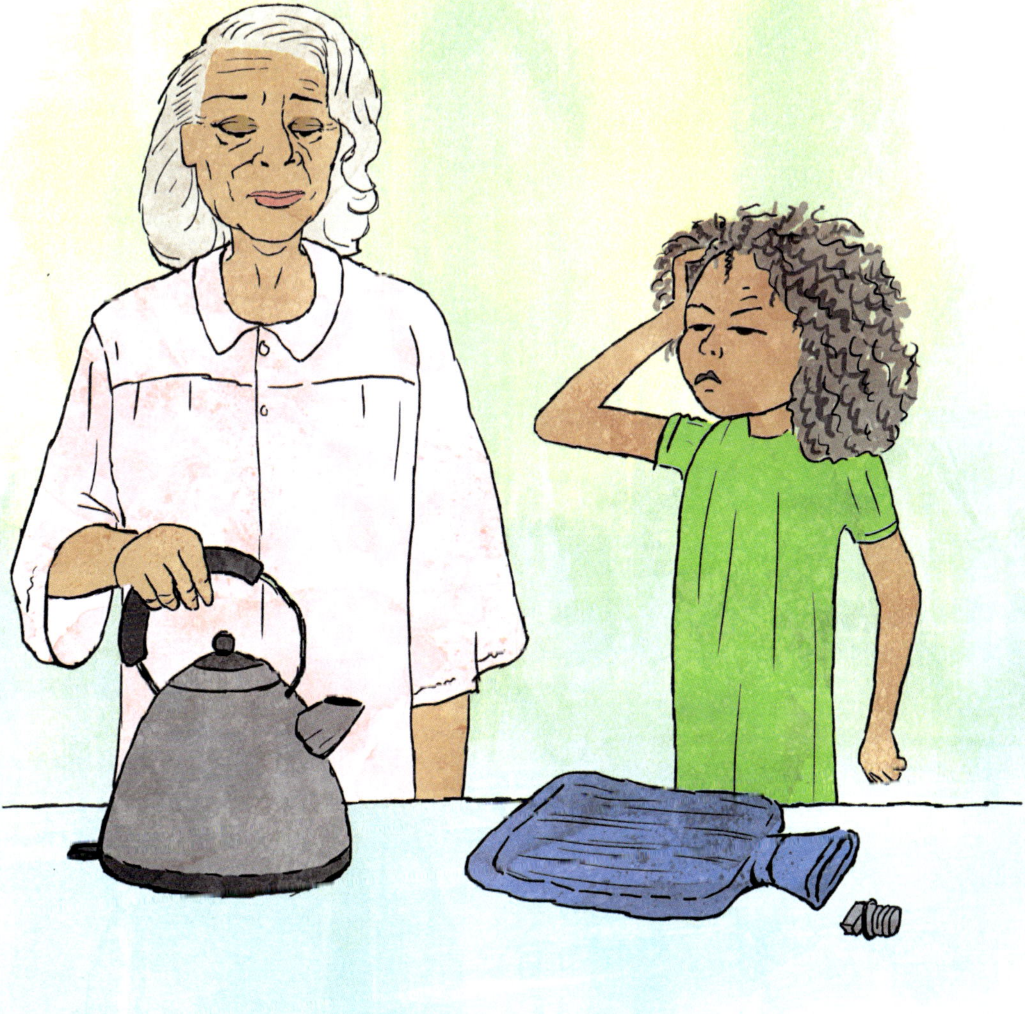

My friends in school all talk about places they have been to like Southport Pleasureland, which isn't far from the Pier. I haven't been there for ages. Some of them had been to Farmer Ted's and I want to go and see those places myself, but I can't.

You see we cannot take Nanna where there would be lots of noise, it would confuse her too much.

Unless it is someone else's birthday party it's impossible to go.

Instead, at the weekend, we do our special trip to Southport with Nanna. Mum told me that it was good for Nanna to go and visit places she knew when she was younger and where there is not so much noise. We don't go on the beach anymore for a paddle or for me to pretend I am a mermaid. We simply go along the promenade and then to the café at the end of the pier.

Nanna loves it. She doesn't get upset or angry when we come here, and she has this little smile to her. It looks like she is somewhere else in her mind.

Sometimes a friend now comes with me and the family to Southport and we leave the grown-ups in the café and explore. It's not easy to bring friends around to our house. It's a small house and, although we can be in my room, we can become noisy and Nanna doesn't like it and she starts to talk to herself and call out to people.

Its easier for me to go around to my friends houses to play but I don't do this as much as I would like to. For a start I want to make sure our house is spick and span clean, so Nanna does not try to tidy it, and then, a lot of the time, I just want to fall asleep, that's just how tired I am.

If I am totally honest with you, I've been feeling a bit low recently. I used to be good at some subjects at school, especially science but I haven't been able to concentrate for being so tired and my marks have gone down the slippery slope. I pretend that I don't care but the thing is, I do care. I love doing well in school but it's just not happening.

I'm also getting jealous of my friends going off and doing this and that. Some days in school that's all I hear, we did this, we did that, and we all had a great time, but I didn't as I wasn't there. All that has made my friends bond with each other more and I want to bond with them more too.

All my friends mean well but the other day we were joking around and pretended to be fairy tale princesses and straightaway they chose that I was Sleeping Beauty. I don't want to be sleeping anything.

But I can't say anything. Can I? After all, its not me who is ill.

One day, Mum picked me up from school and said we were going to meet someone at our house. Her name was Michelle from Sefton Carers. I thought she had come around to chat to Mum about Nanna, but she had come to speak to Mum about me!

Mum and Dad had spoken to my teacher at parents evening. I was worried about them all meeting up as I sort of did not tell Mum and Dad that my schoolwork was suffering, and I was almost sleepwalking around the place.

I thought I was going to get into a lot of trouble.

I was wrong.

Michelle was all smiles and wanted to chat to me about all the stuff I did at home, like helping clean and all that. She asked me about how did this affect me in school and it was quite hard at first as Mum was in the room but then Mum said that they knew that I wasn't doing well in school and they knew it was because I was doing so much at home, looking after Nanna.

Well that was a turn up for the books. I was shocked. Mum was so sorry about things and apologised to me. She said that I was the most important person in the house and that I should enjoy my childhood as much as possible. She was sorry that I had to do so much around the house, but I said that I wanted to as I love Nanna, and Mum and Dad.

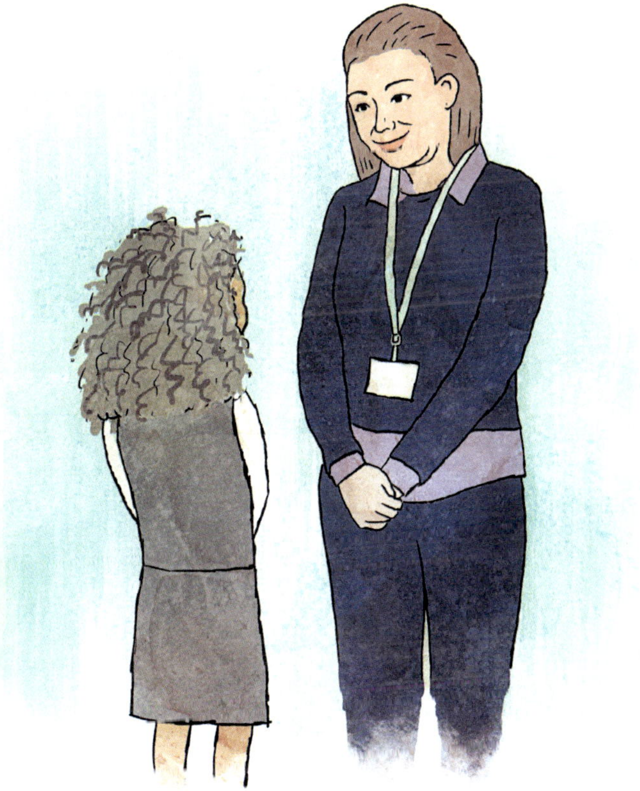

Michelle asked me how it affected other things like hanging around with my friends. I didn't really want to answer this question. I didn't want Mum or Dad to know how low I was feeling about not having time to spend with my friends. I didn't want them to think I was selfish.

But I did tell them, and Michelle told me that I was not the only child to look after someone at home. She told me that there were other children my age and even younger who have to do similar stuff for their parents or their brothers and sisters too. She also told me that these other children suffered in school and with their friends because of all the care they gave to others and that it was only natural to feel a bit down.

Wow. I felt a great weight came off my shoulders. Firstly, I thought it was just me but to hear there were others and that I wasn't selfish made me feel a lot better.

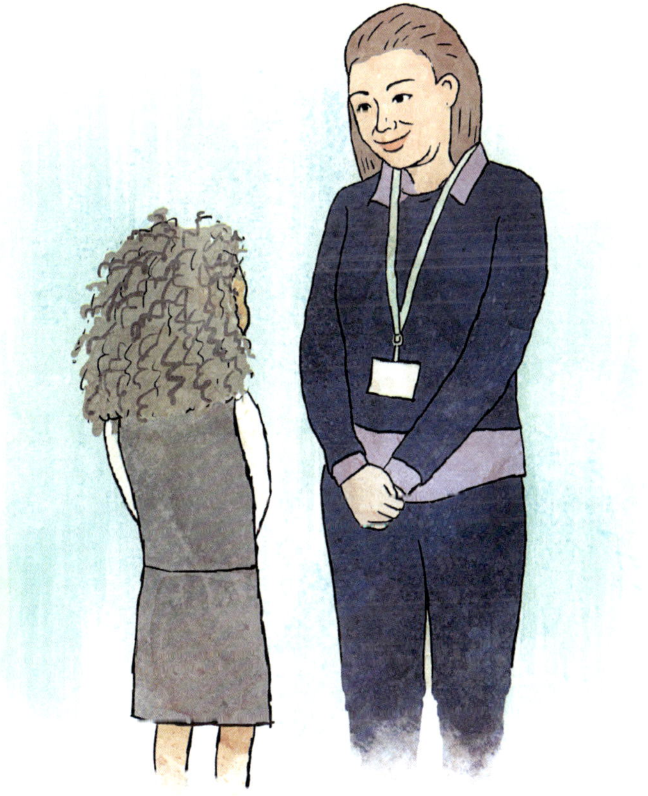

Michelle asked me how it affected other things like hanging around with my friends. I didn't really want to answer this question. I didn't want Mum or Dad to know how low I was feeling about not having time to spend with my friends. I didn't want them to think I was selfish.

But I did tell them, and Michelle told me that I was not the only child to look after someone at home. She told me that there were other children my age and even younger who have to do similar stuff for their parents or their brothers and sisters too. She also told me that these other children suffered in school and with their friends because of all the care they gave to others and that it was only natural to feel a bit down.

Wow. I felt a great weight came off my shoulders. Firstly, I thought it was just me but to hear there were others and that I wasn't selfish made me feel a lot better.

Michelle told me that I was called a young carer and that she and others from Sefton Carers were here to look after all the young carers they knew about.

She told me that it was hard to find all the young carers out there in the world and that it was only after parents evening that they got to hear about me. She said that some young carers go unnoticed and are unaware of the help they can receive.

For a start, I met up with my Headteacher and he said school would support me. He still wanted me to take part in lessons and do as much as I could but he realised that I was doing so much in the day and night that I was to be allowed some time out so I could just relax and gather my thoughts or talk to a member of staff.

For the past month I have been going to a weekly youth club with Michelle and lots of other young carers. I've not really seen myself as a carer before, but I guess that I am.

I am so glad I can speak to others who look after their Nannas and their Granddads and other members of their family. We've been sharing ideas and tips to help each other out and we all have similar stories to tell. My friends from school understand too. They realise I do stuff that they would never dream of having to do and that it is nice to have others who do the same to talk to.

And that's the thing. I am still caring for Nanna, I told Mum I would not want to change that. It's just now I have my support in place, carers caring for me, if you like.

Last week all the young carers went on a day trip to Blackpool Beach Pleasure Beach. It was absolutely brilliant. We went on the Big One, the big dipper, the dodgems and the Ghost train and all the others we were allowed on.

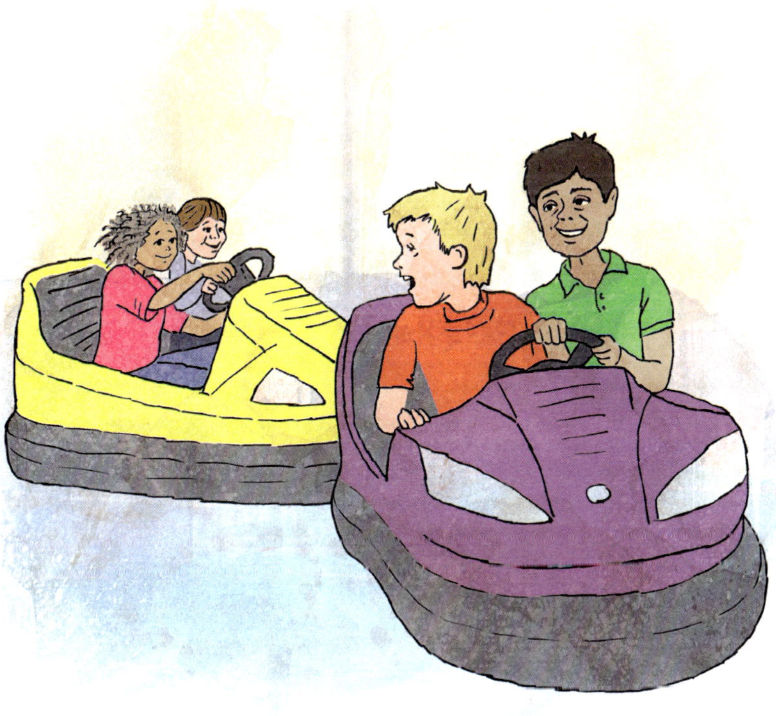

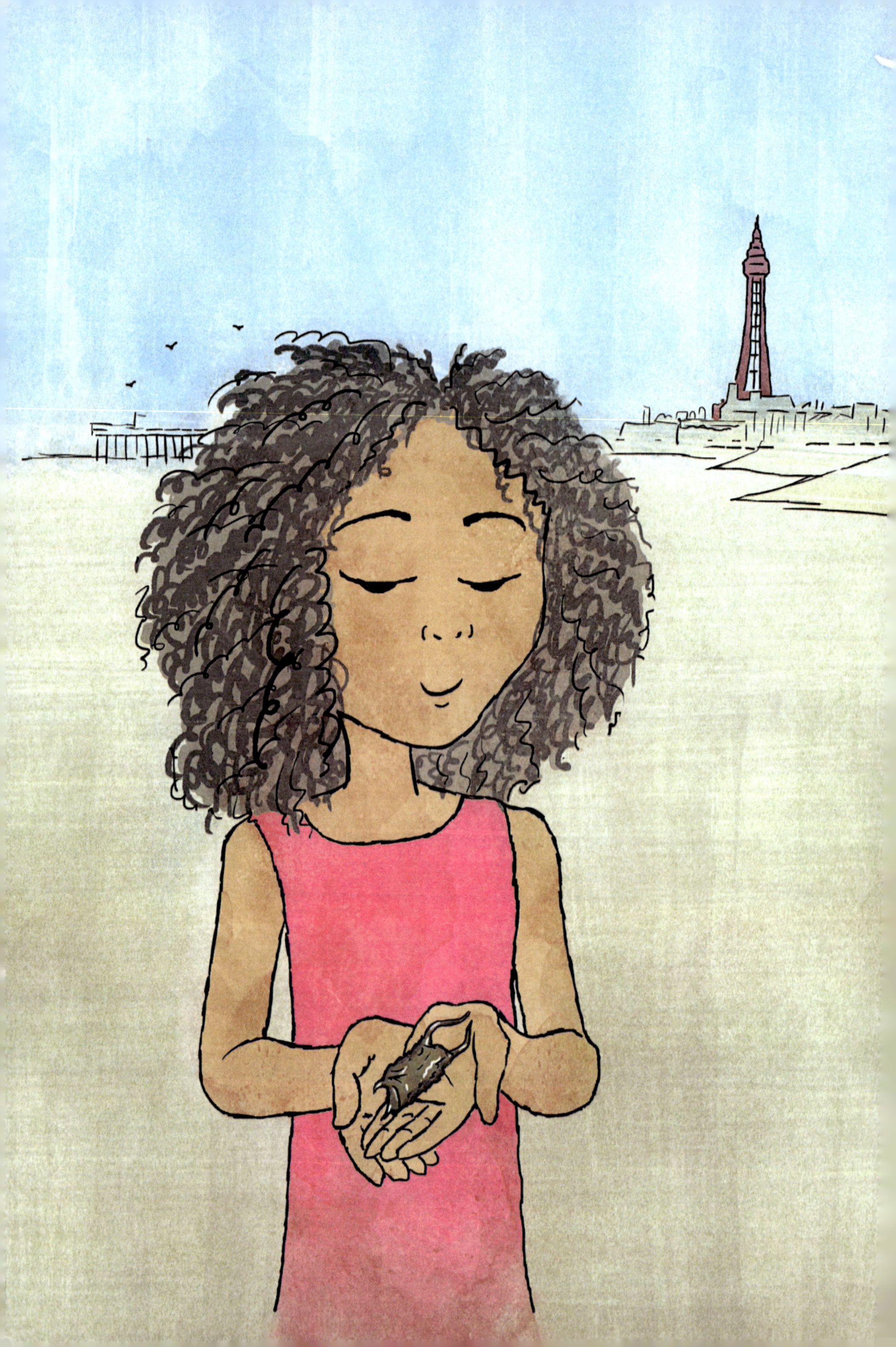

At the end of the day, just before we left, I went for a walk on the beach and thought about the wonderful time I had and that, soon, it would be just a memory.

And this made me think about Nanna and her memories of Southport promenade and pier.

I checked to see if anyone was watching and when I saw that they weren't I wiggled like a mermaid.

I will always be her mermaid and care for her.

Some of the other young carers joined me and it felt good to not be alone.

As we walked back to the bus, I found, on the beach, a mermaid's purse. I picked it up and kept it as a keepsake of all my memories of Nanna.

A Note from Sefton Carers and Charles Lea

Many people helped us write this story. Without their support, advice and time we would simply not have been able to have written this story in a way to reflect the true experiences of young carers.

We thank the following for their help:

Greenbank High School Young Carers Group

Holy Family High School Young Carers Group

Sefton Young Carers North & South Youth Clubs

Steve Morgan Foundation

Mersey Care

Sefton MBC

Clatterbridge Cancer Centre

Sefton Library Service